Northwoods Boathouse Coloring Book

by Glennan Keldin

Alamo Placita Group, LLC
2166 S. Washington St.
Denver, Co 80210

I0419360

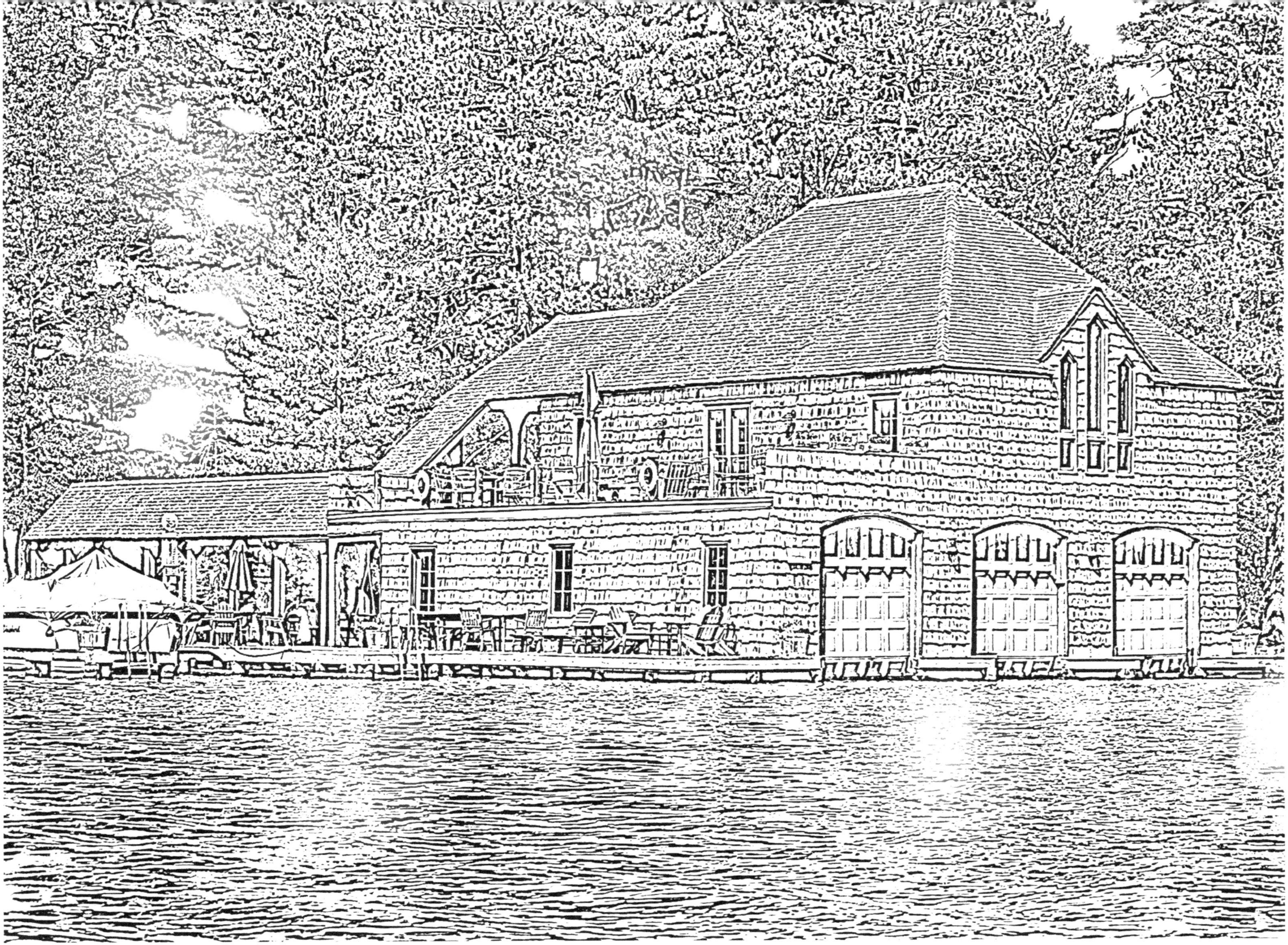

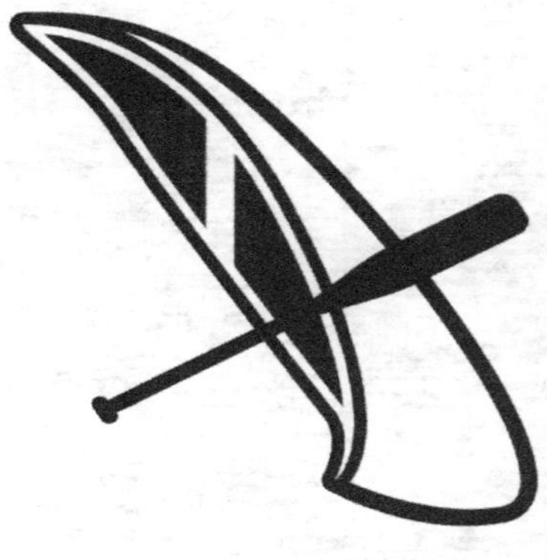

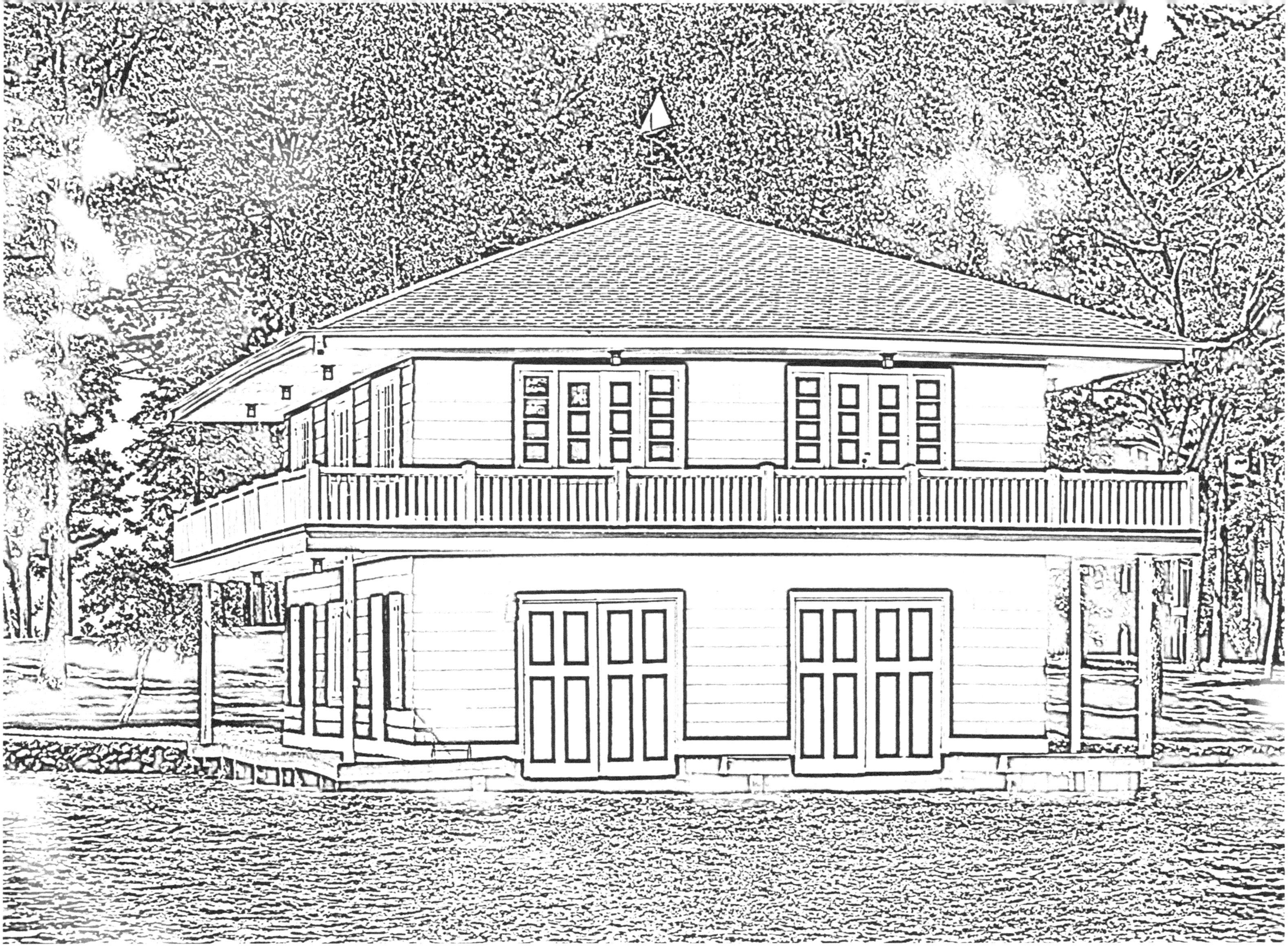

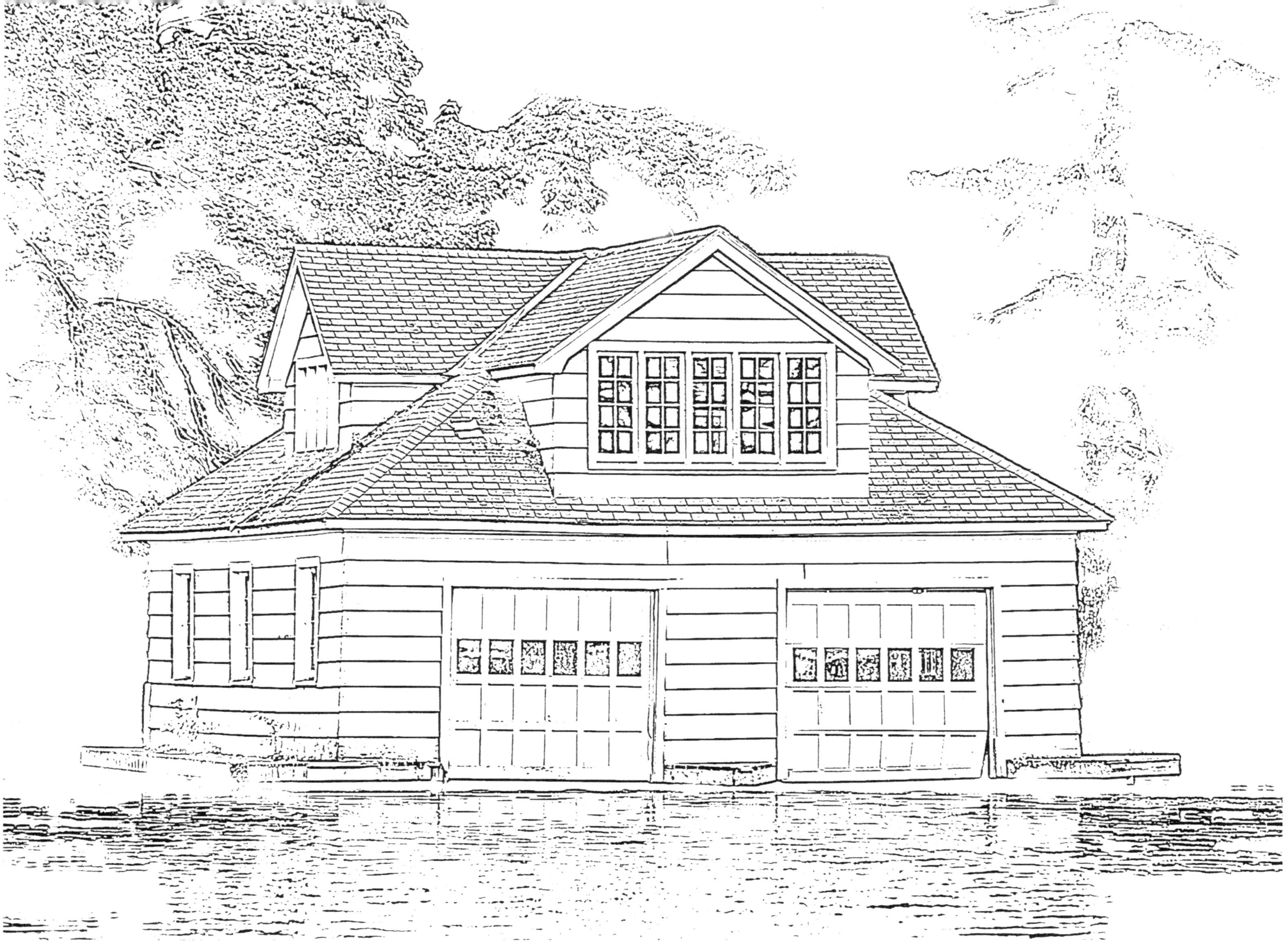

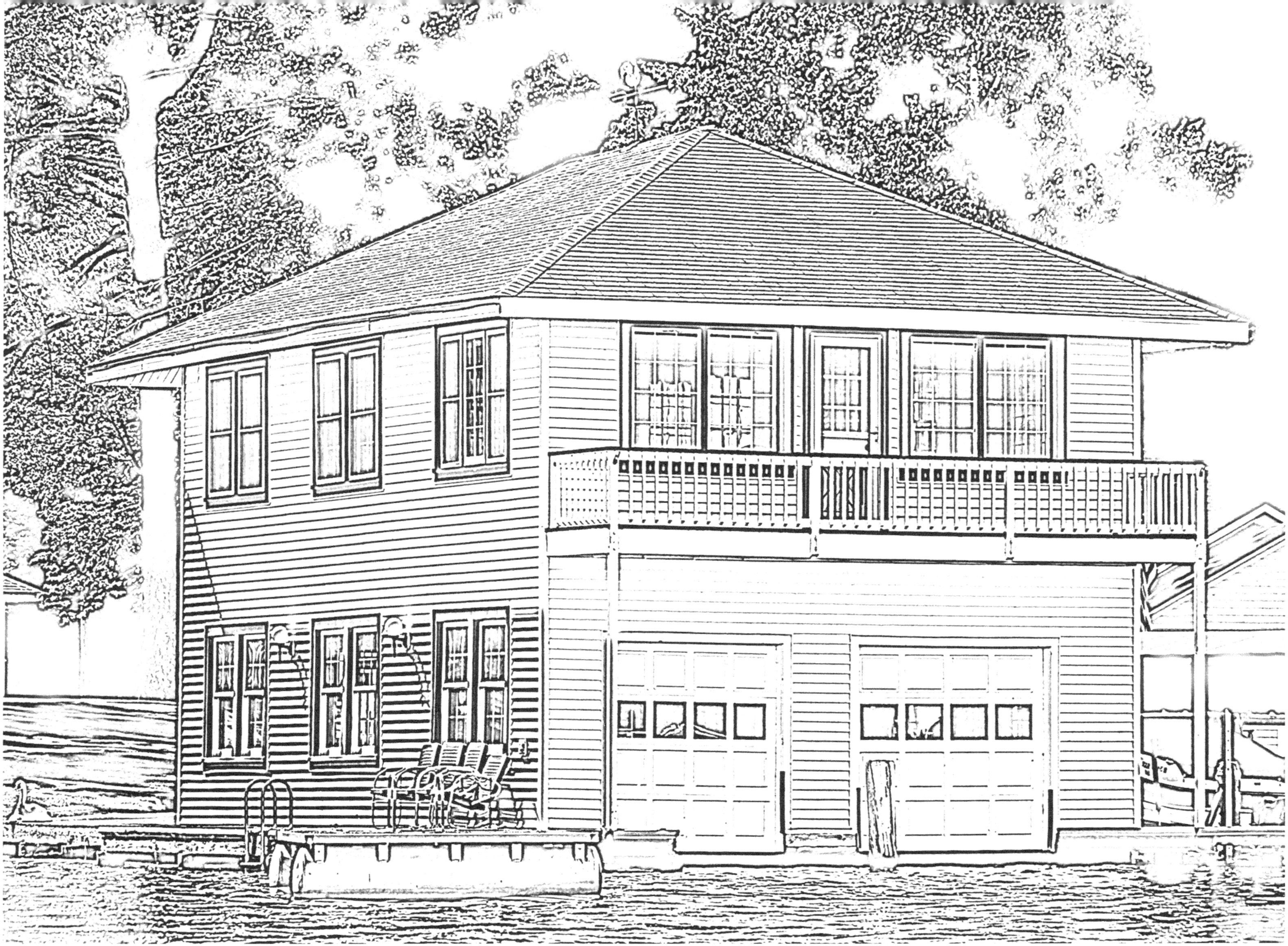

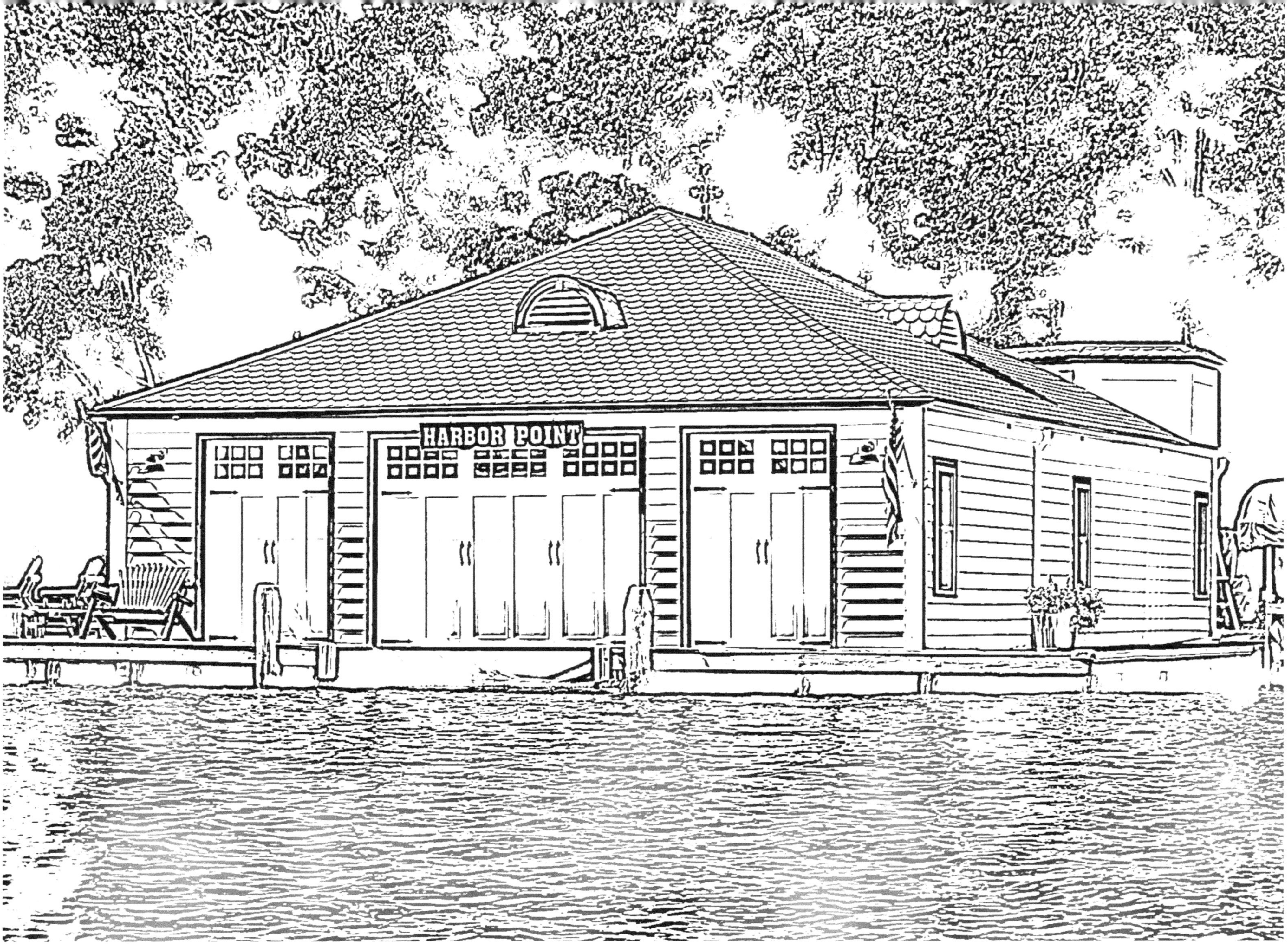
HARBOR POINT

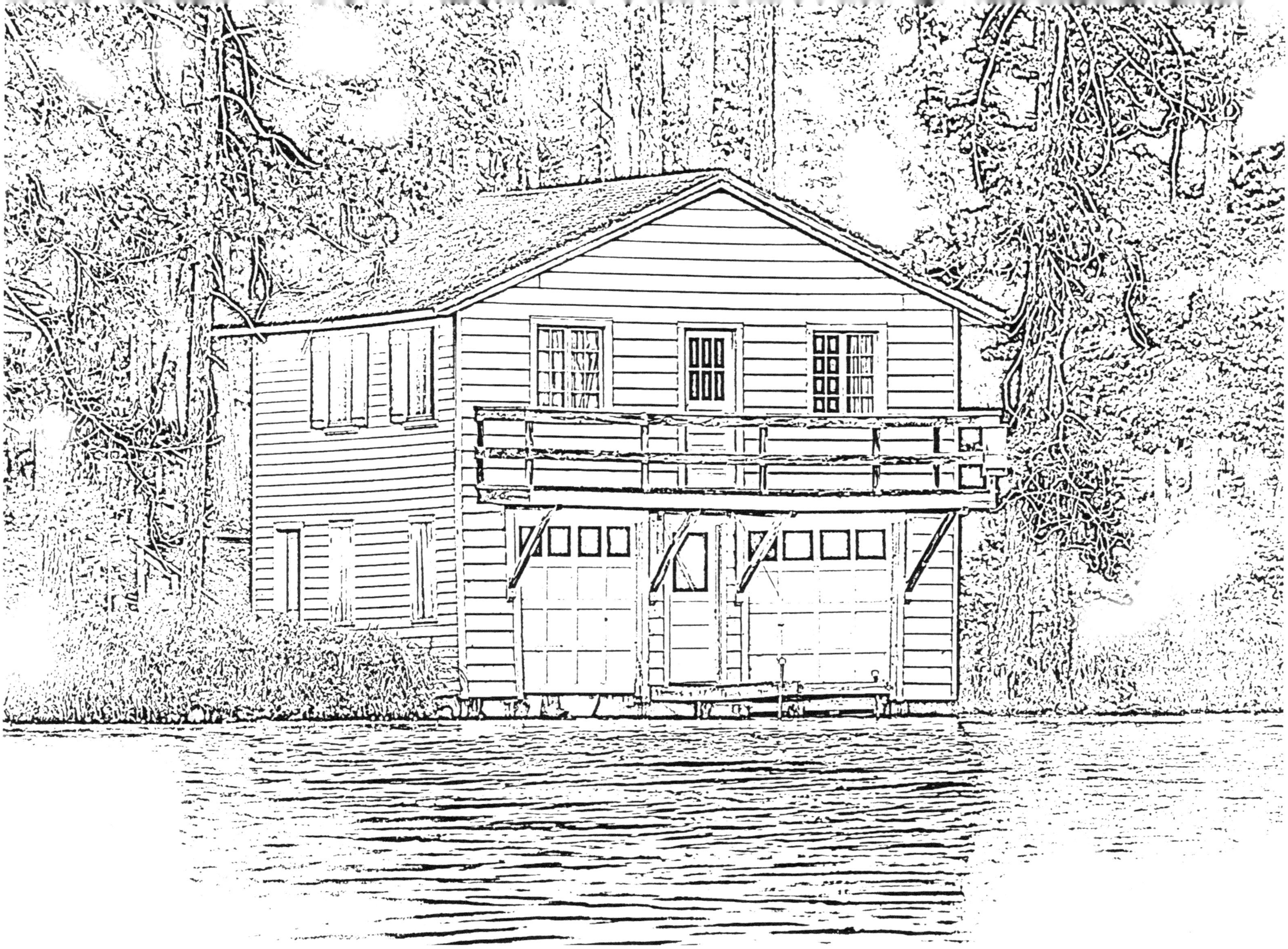

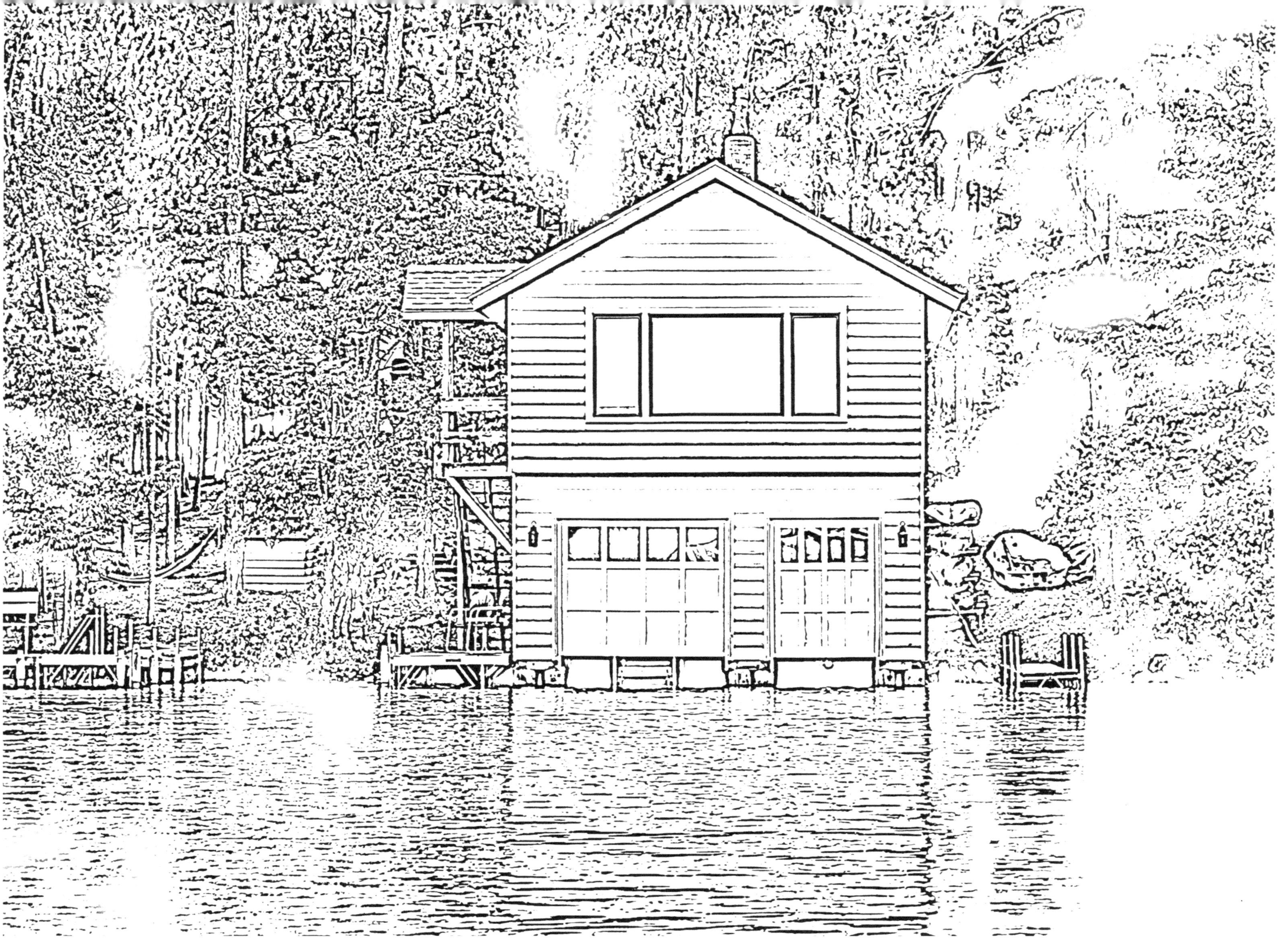

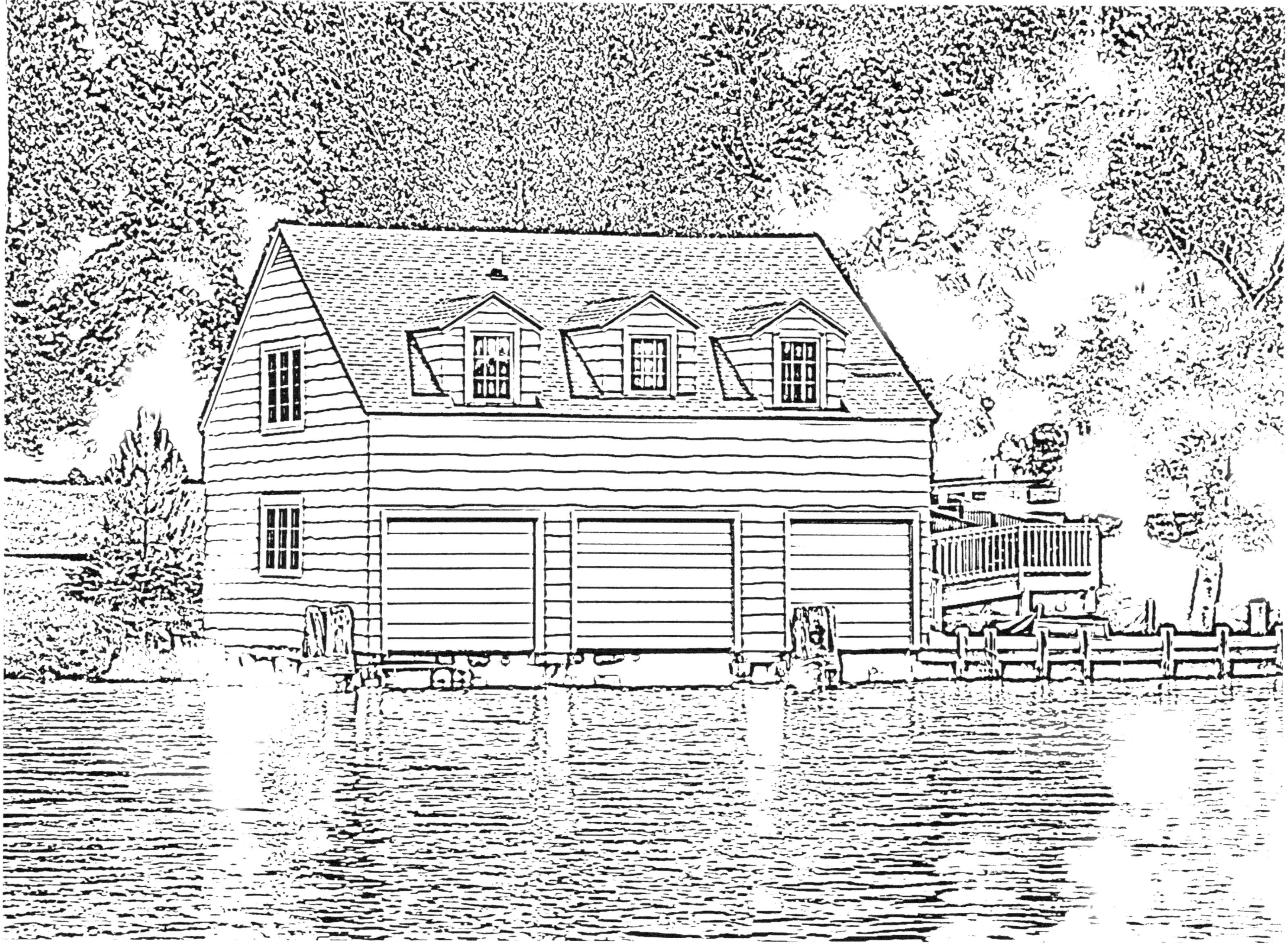

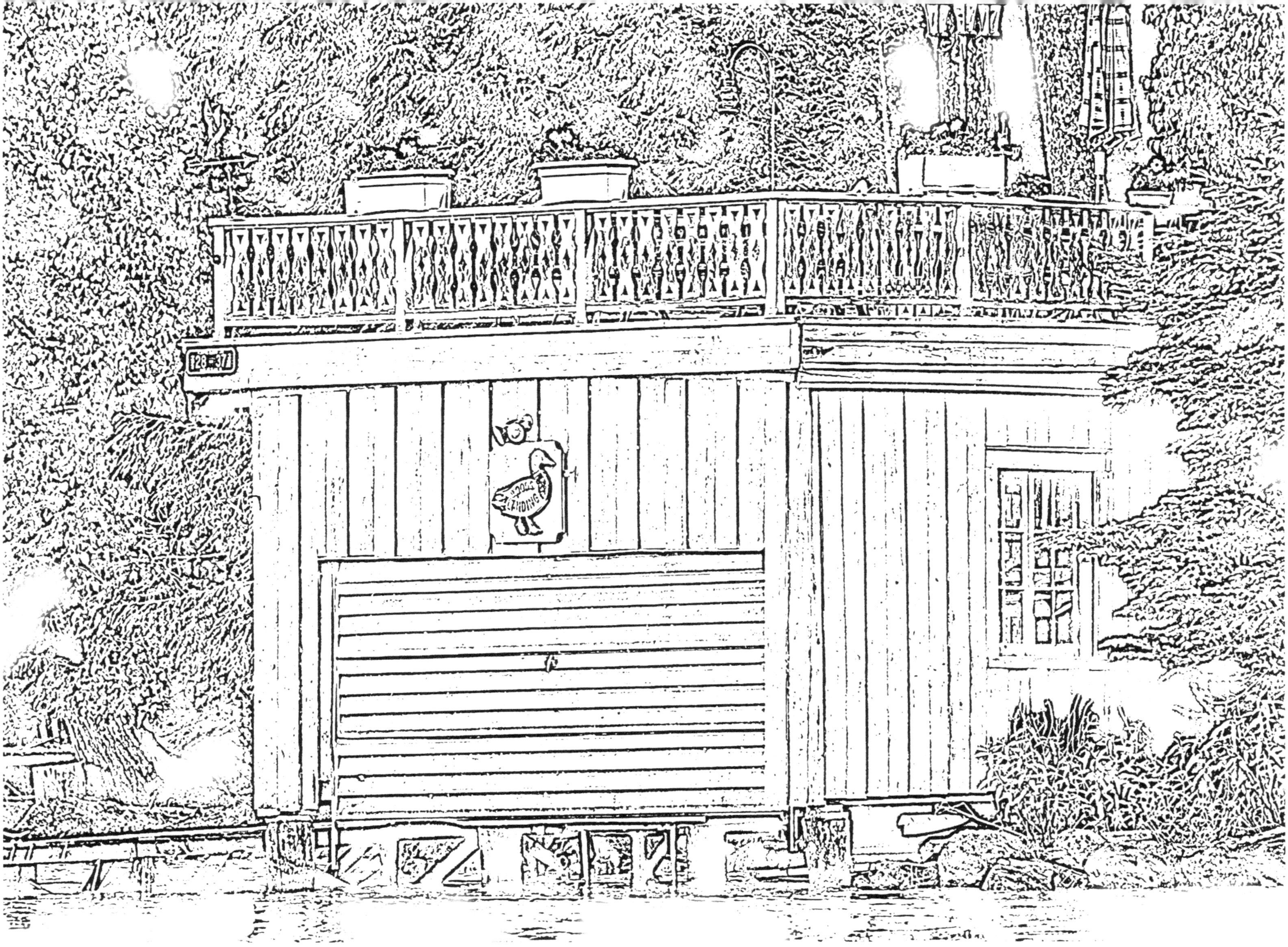
LANDING

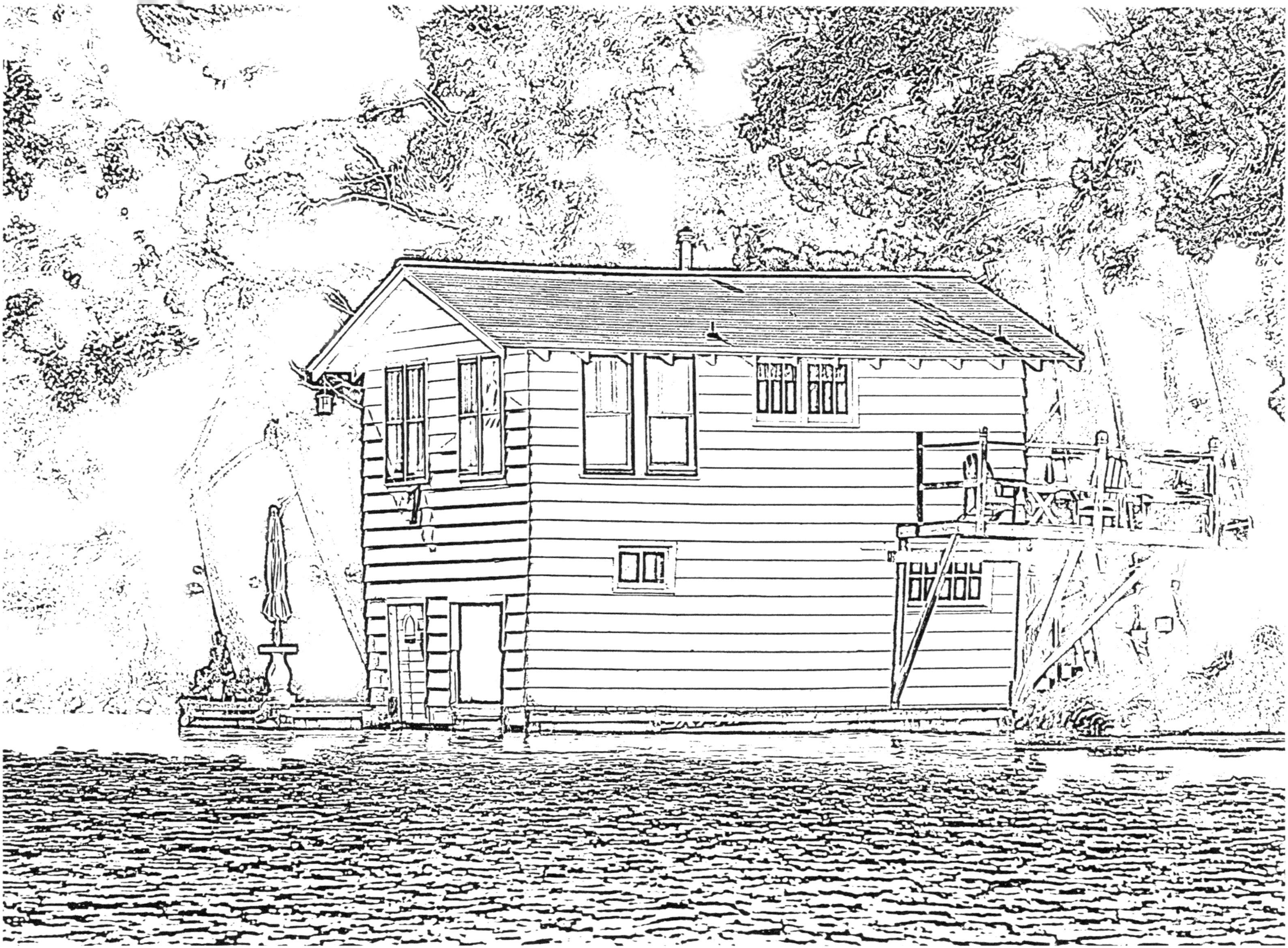

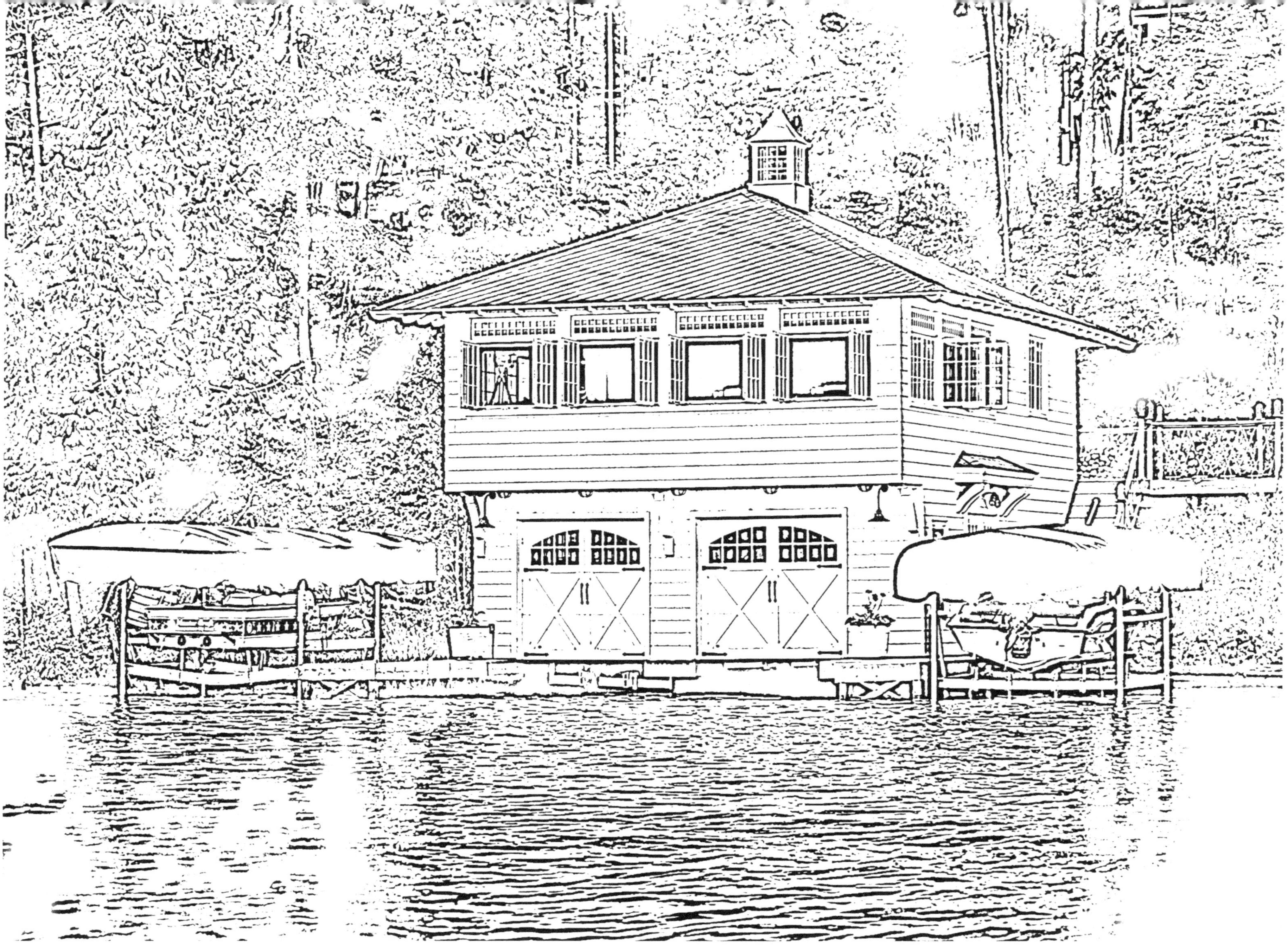

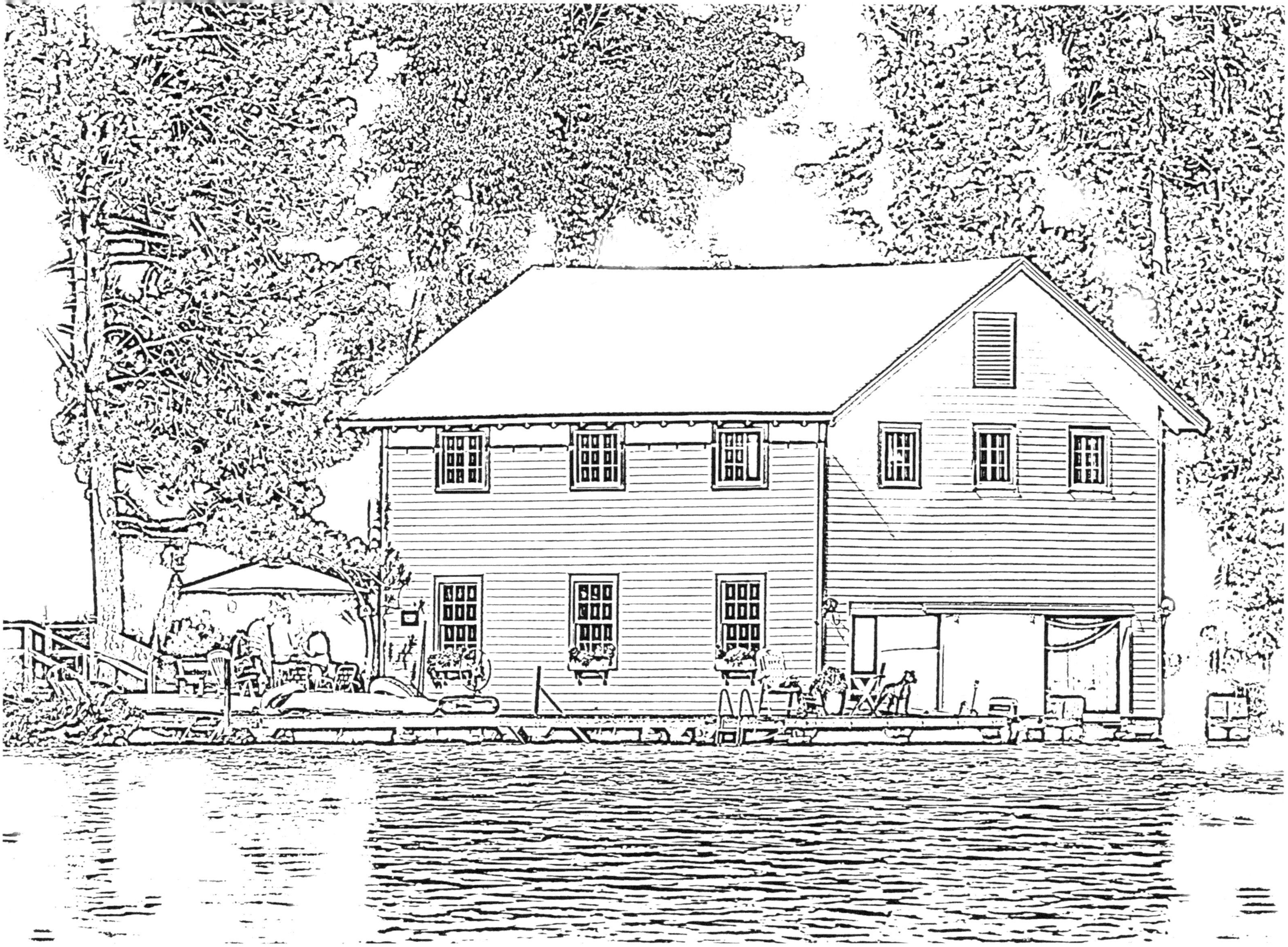

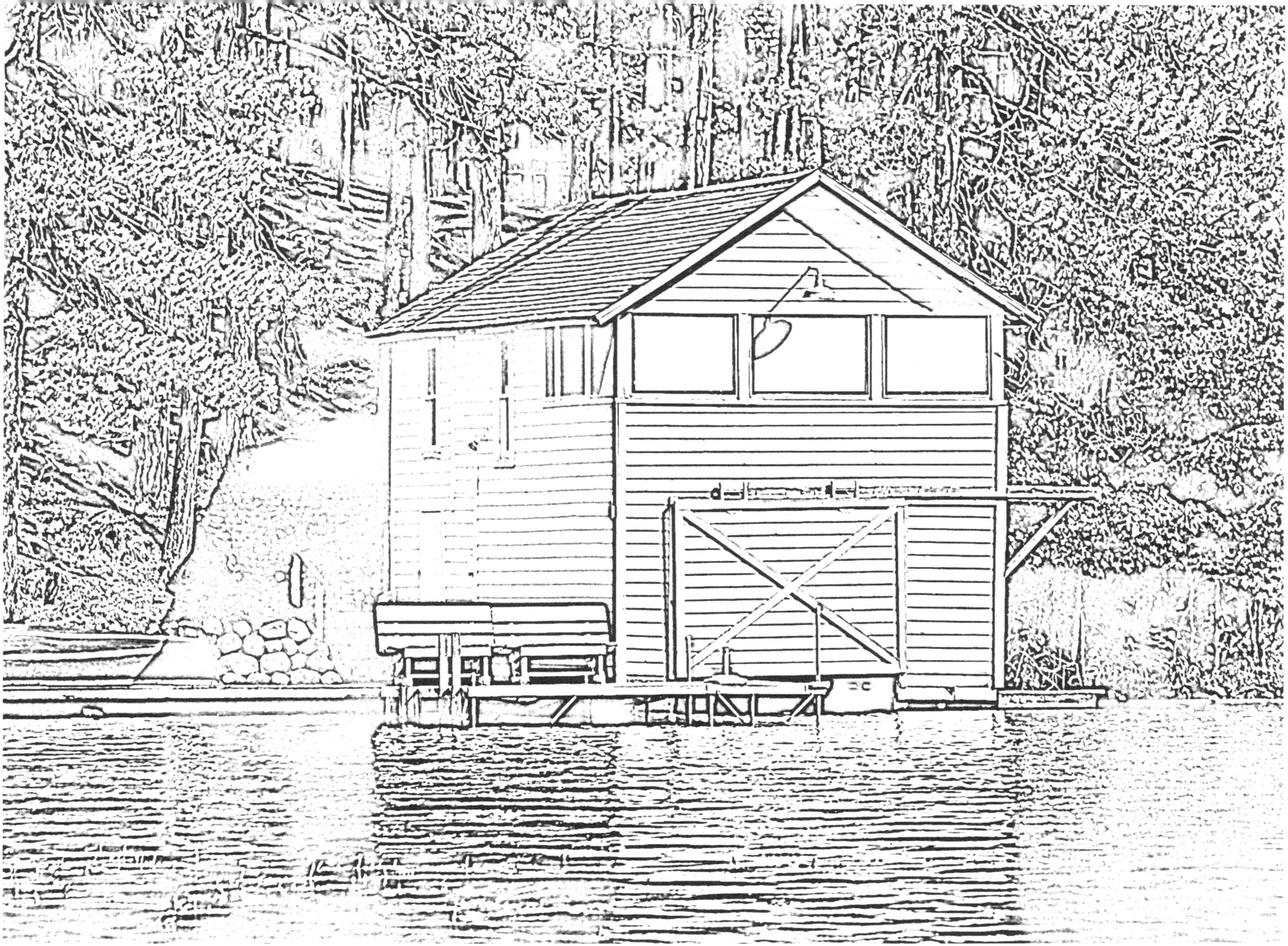

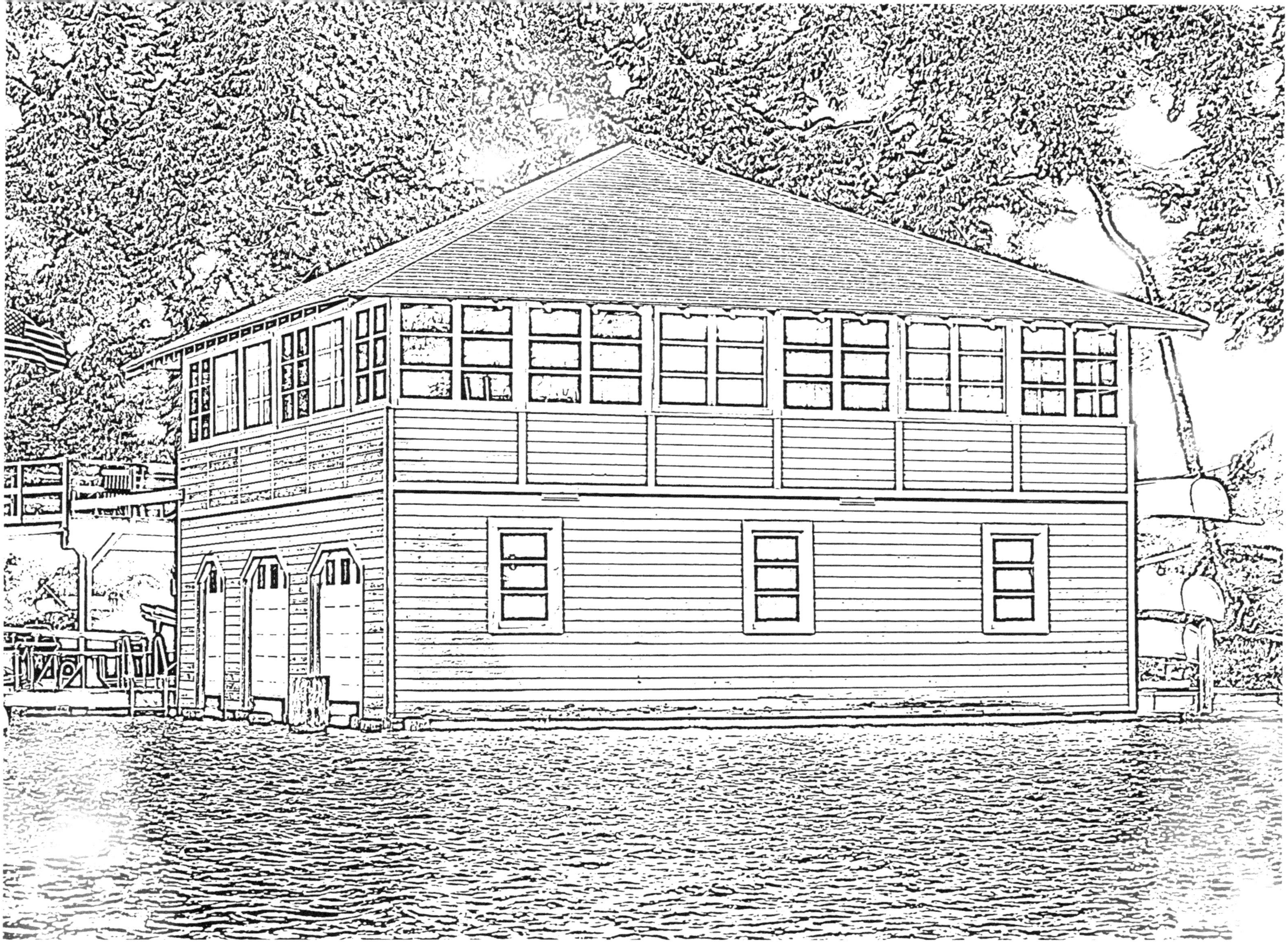

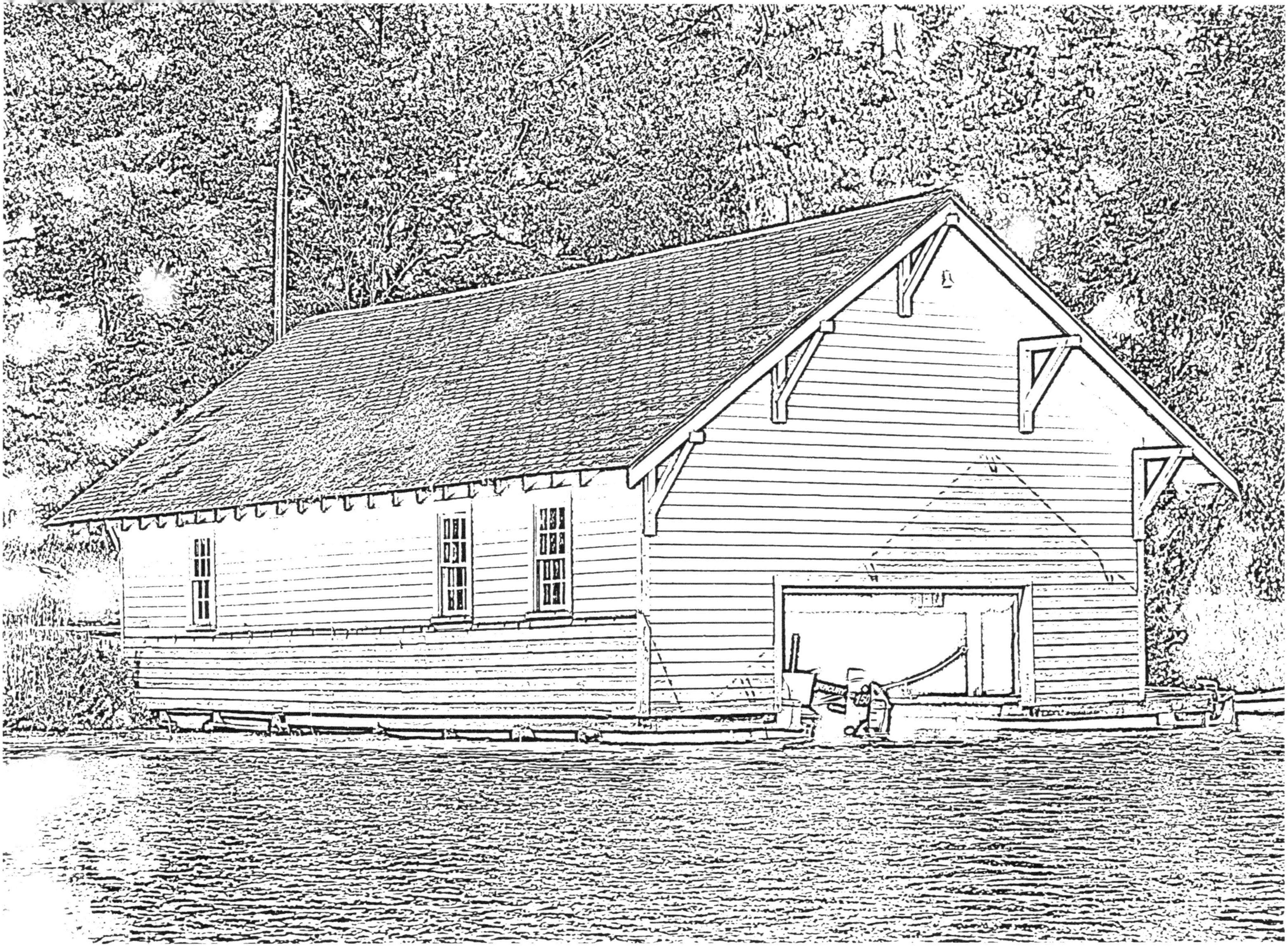

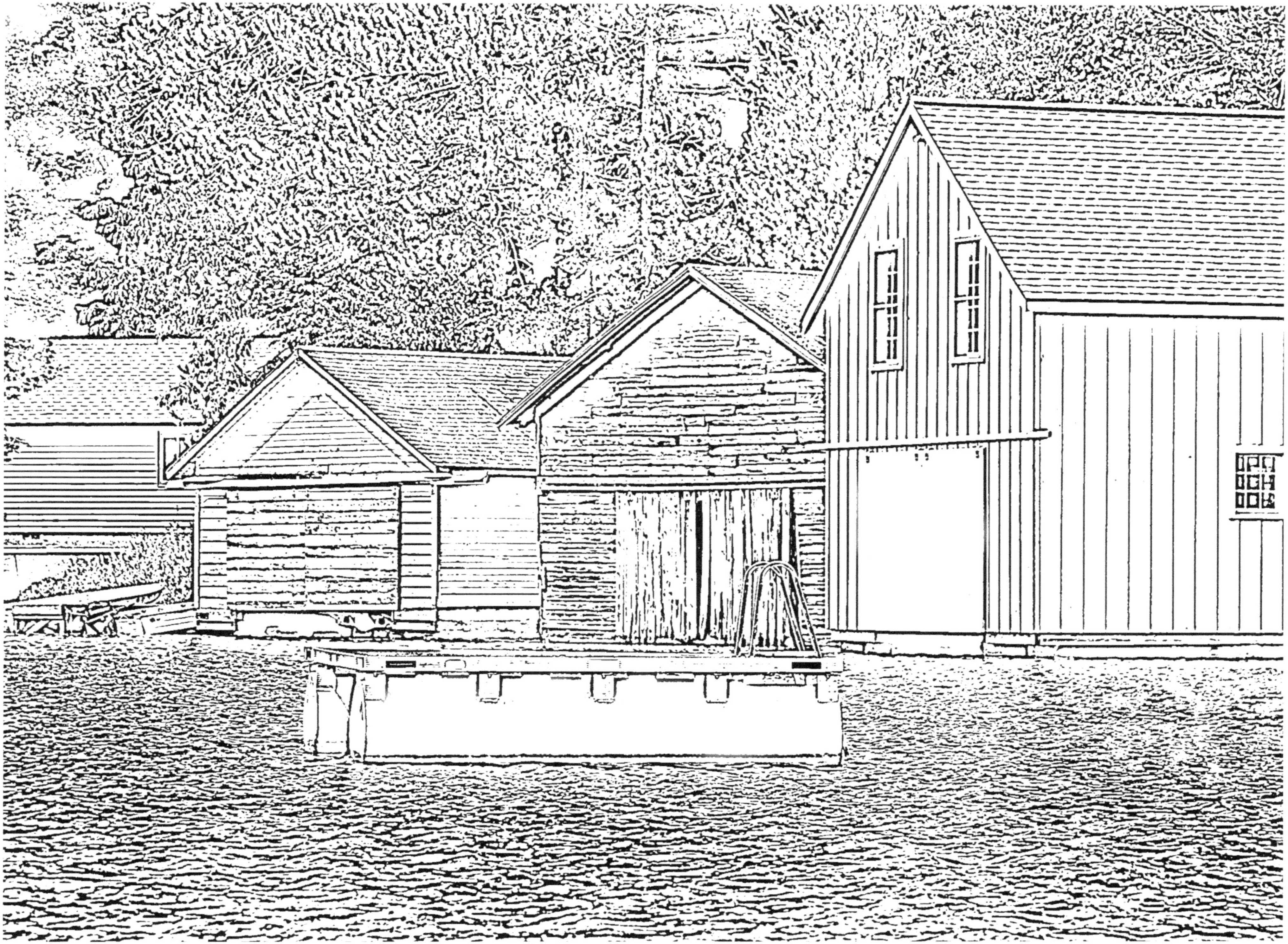

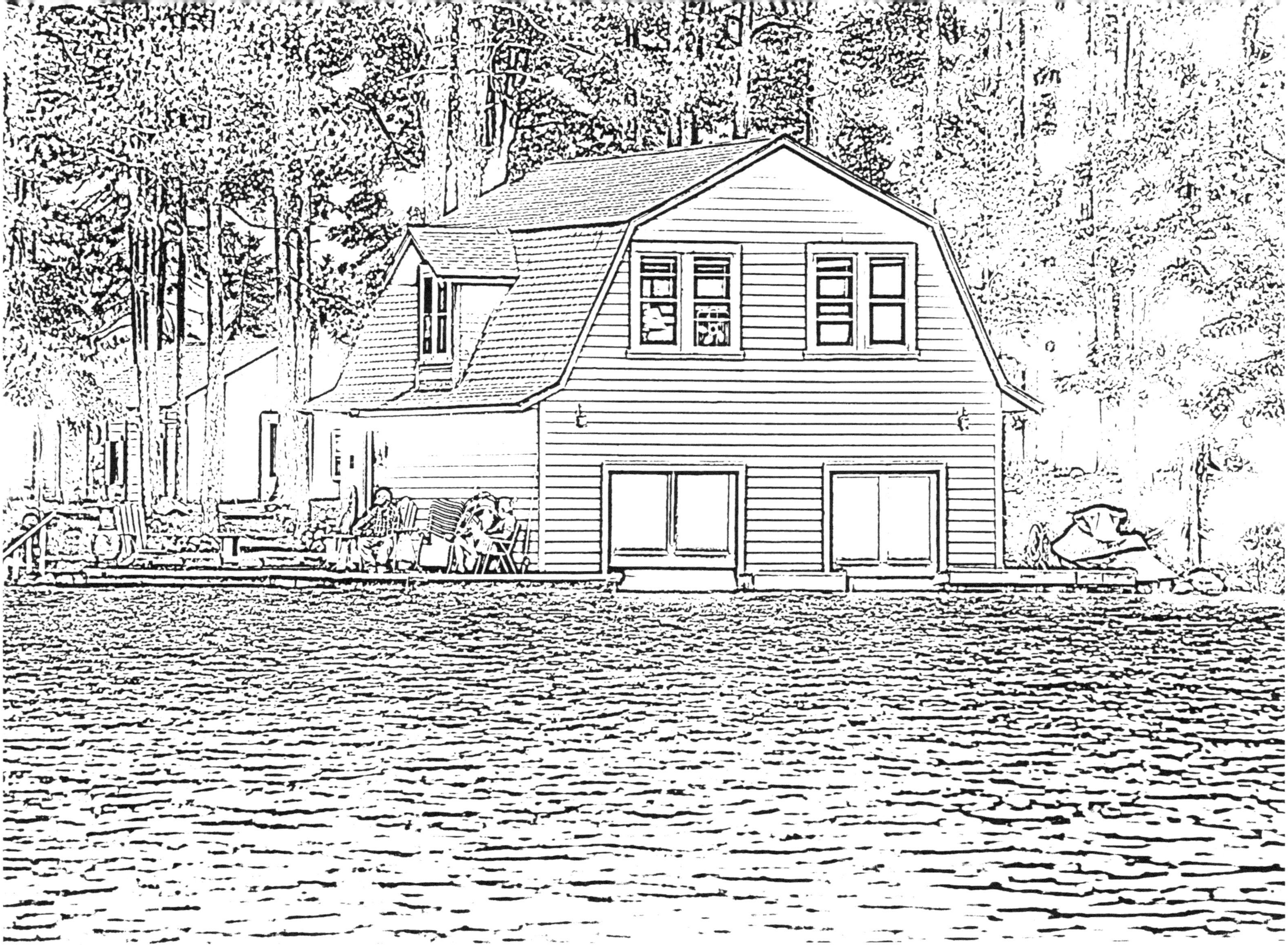

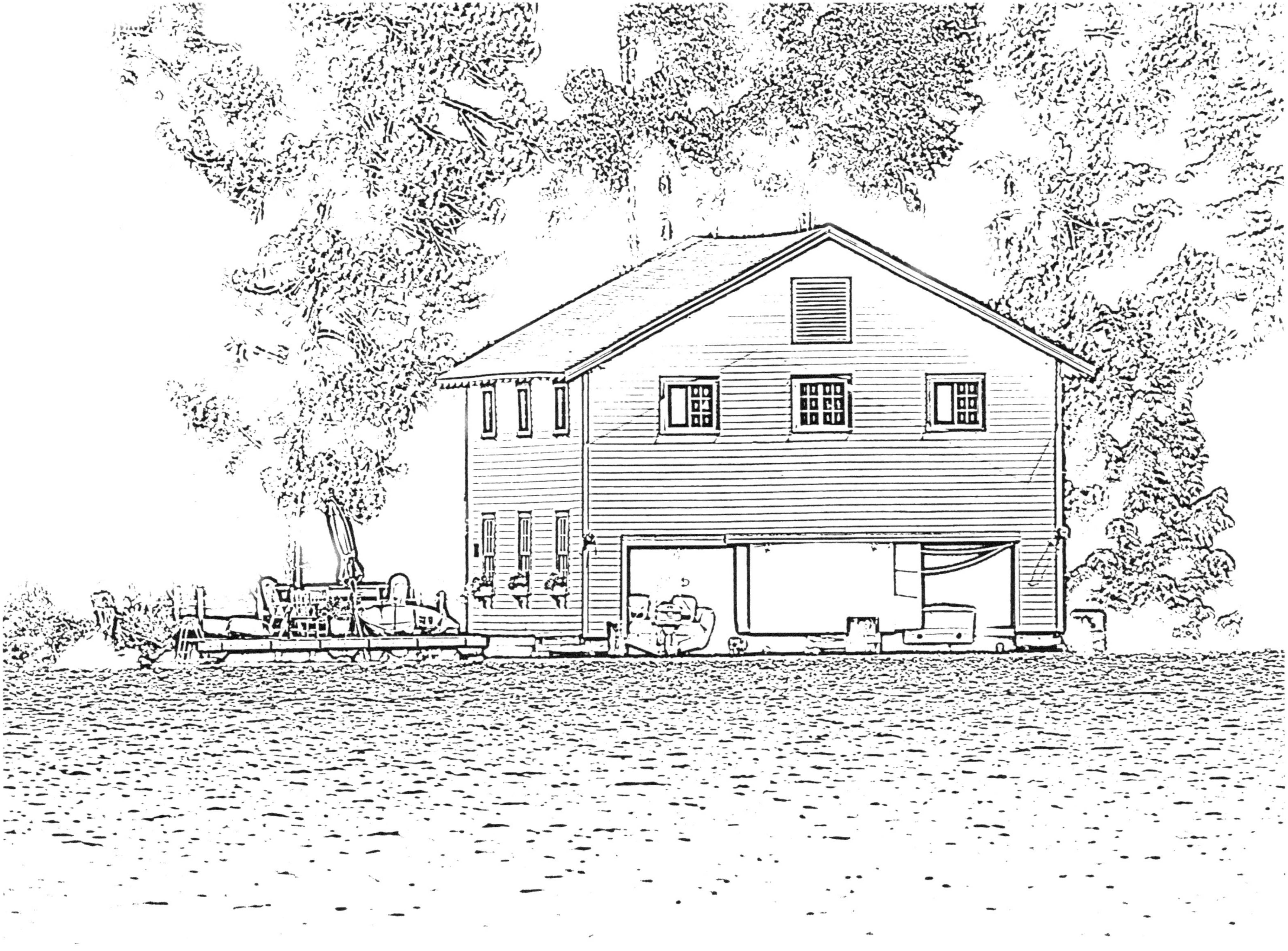

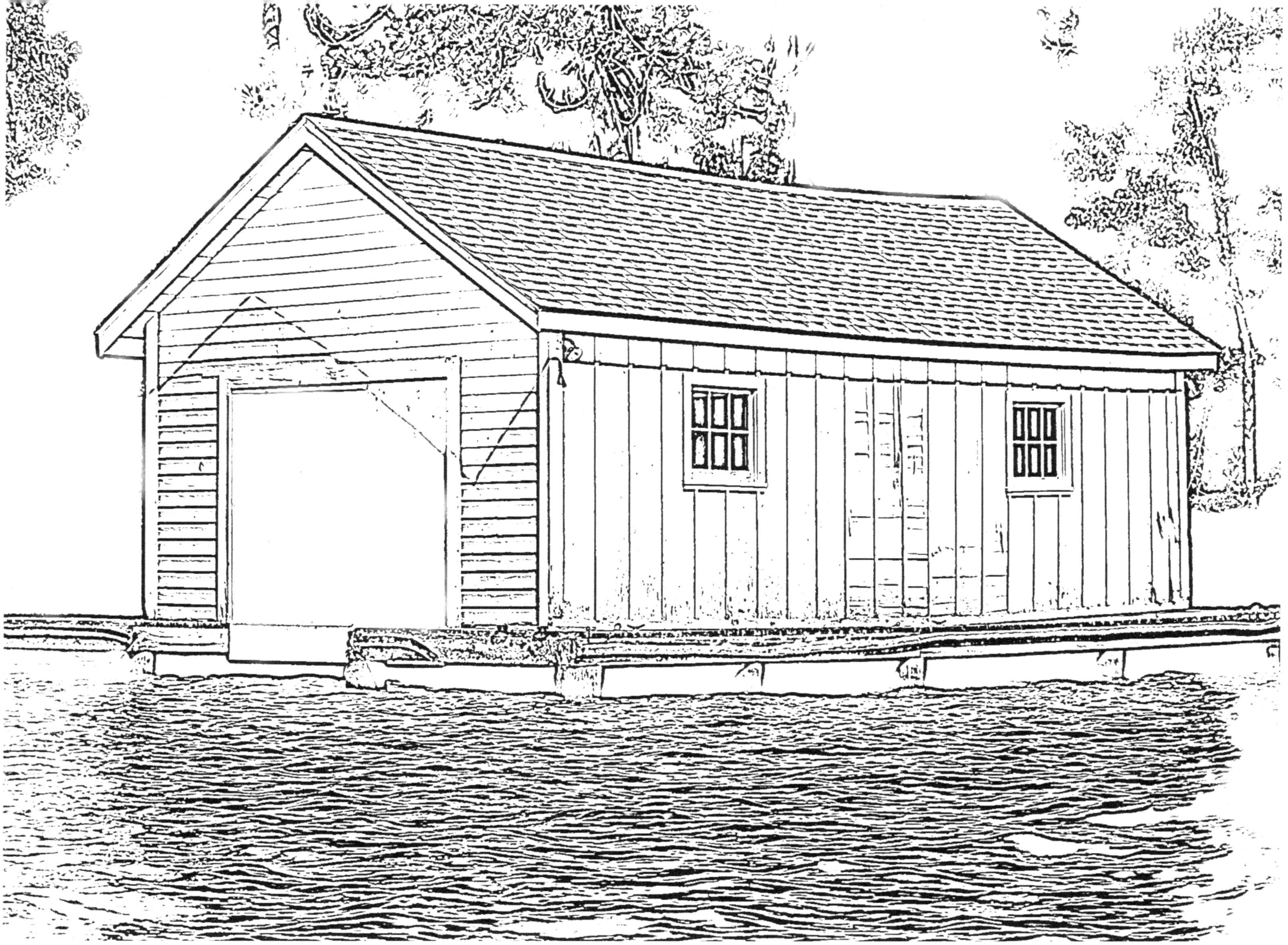

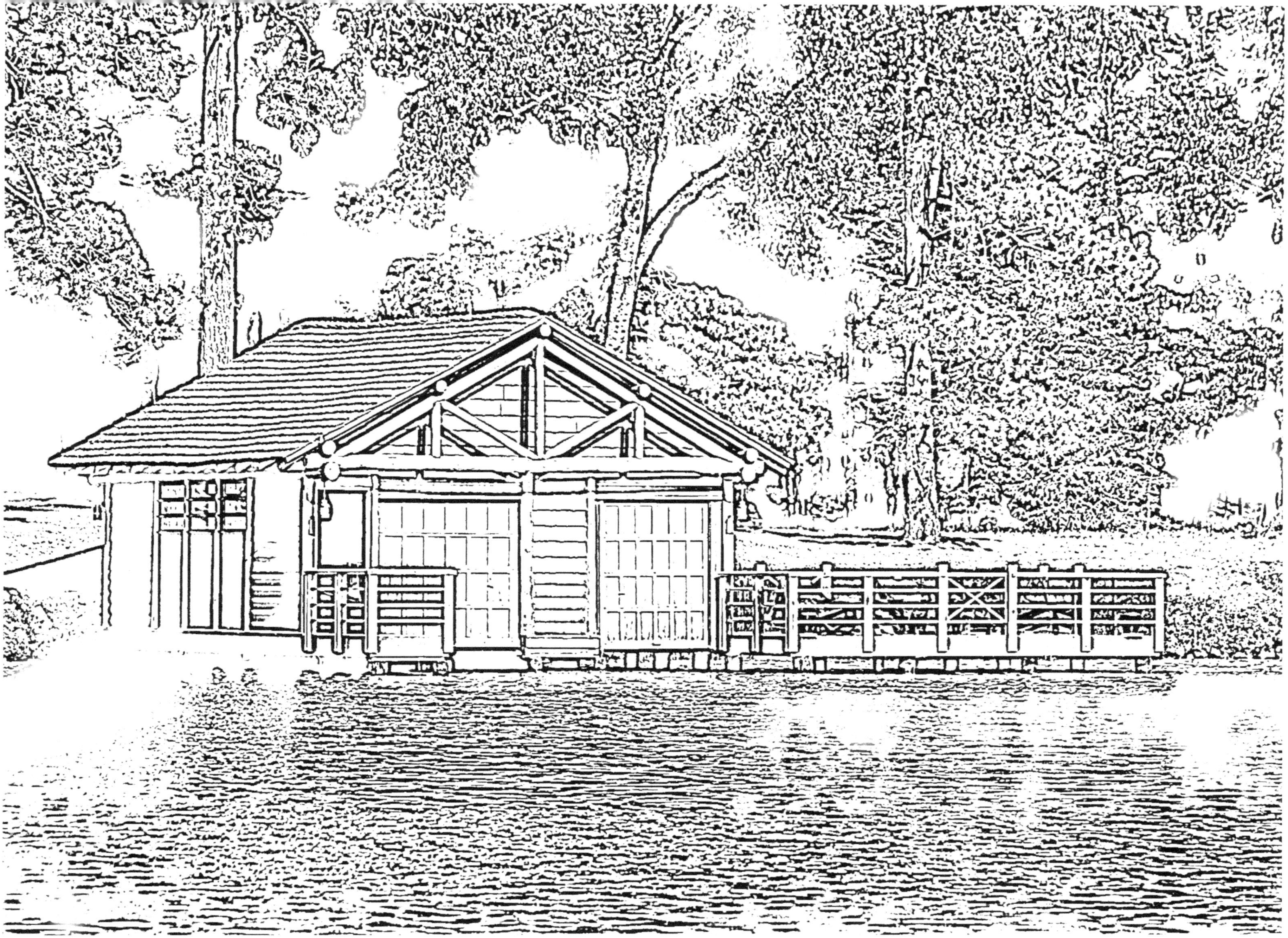

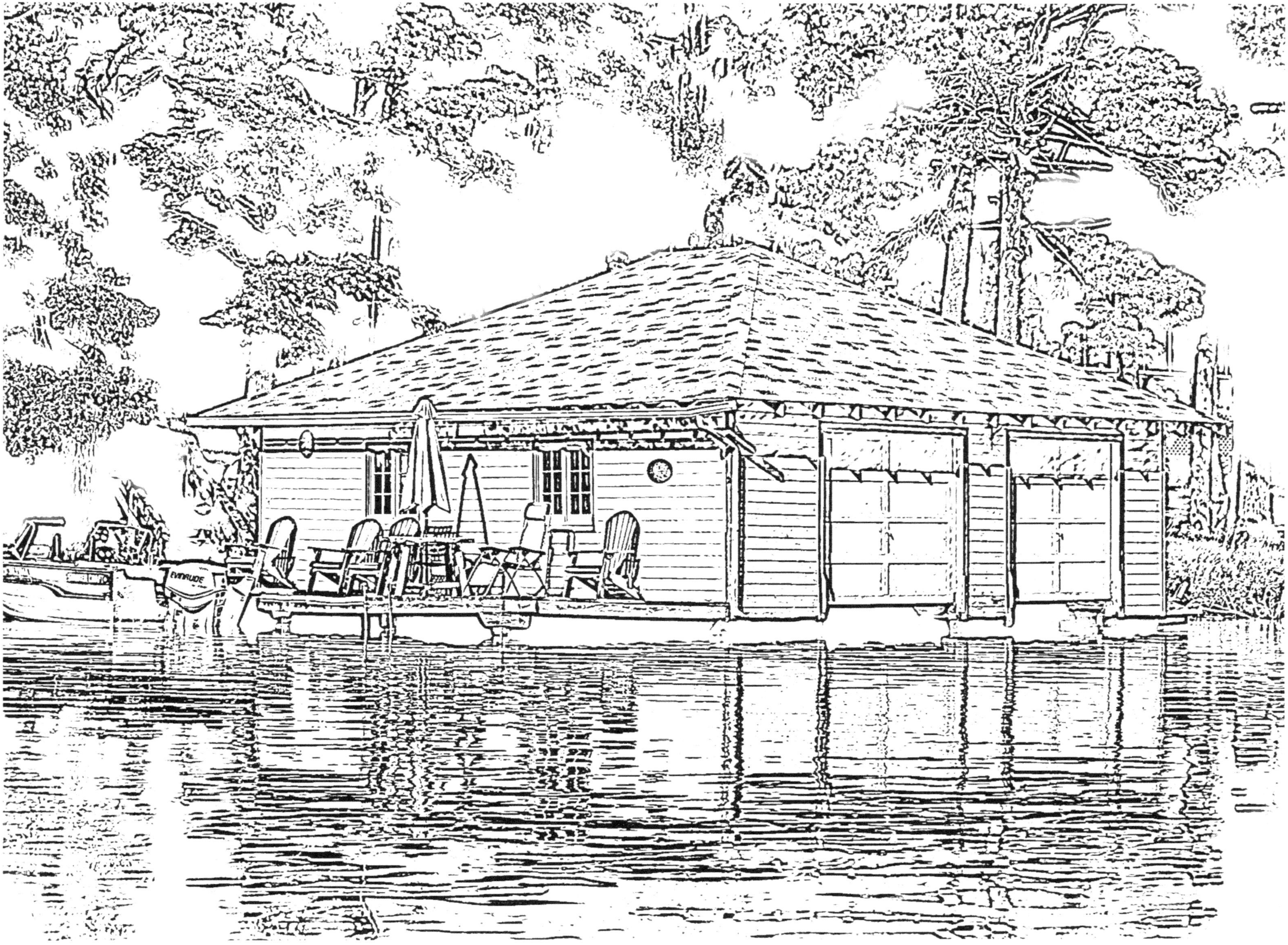
EVINRUDE

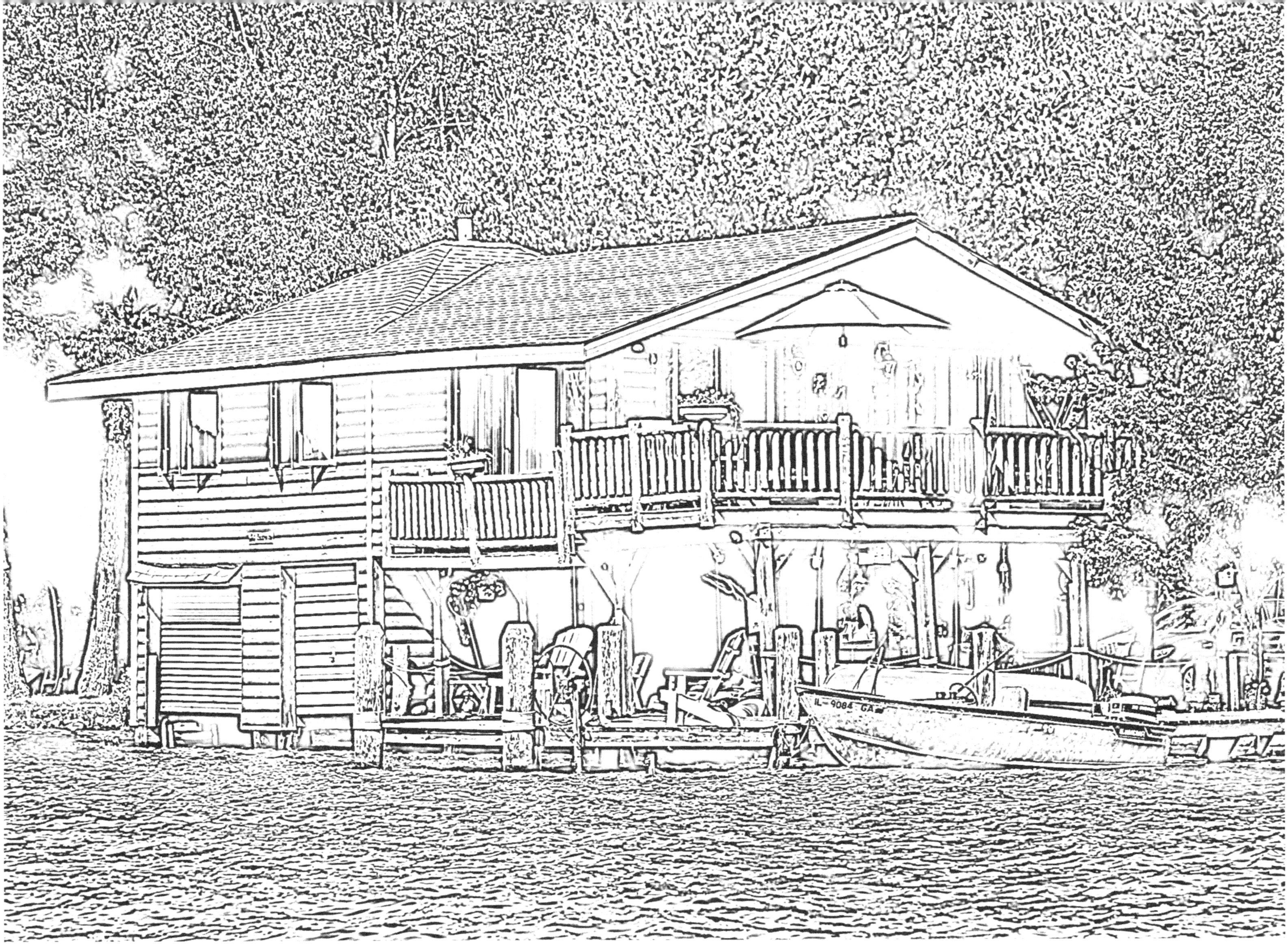
IL-9084 GA

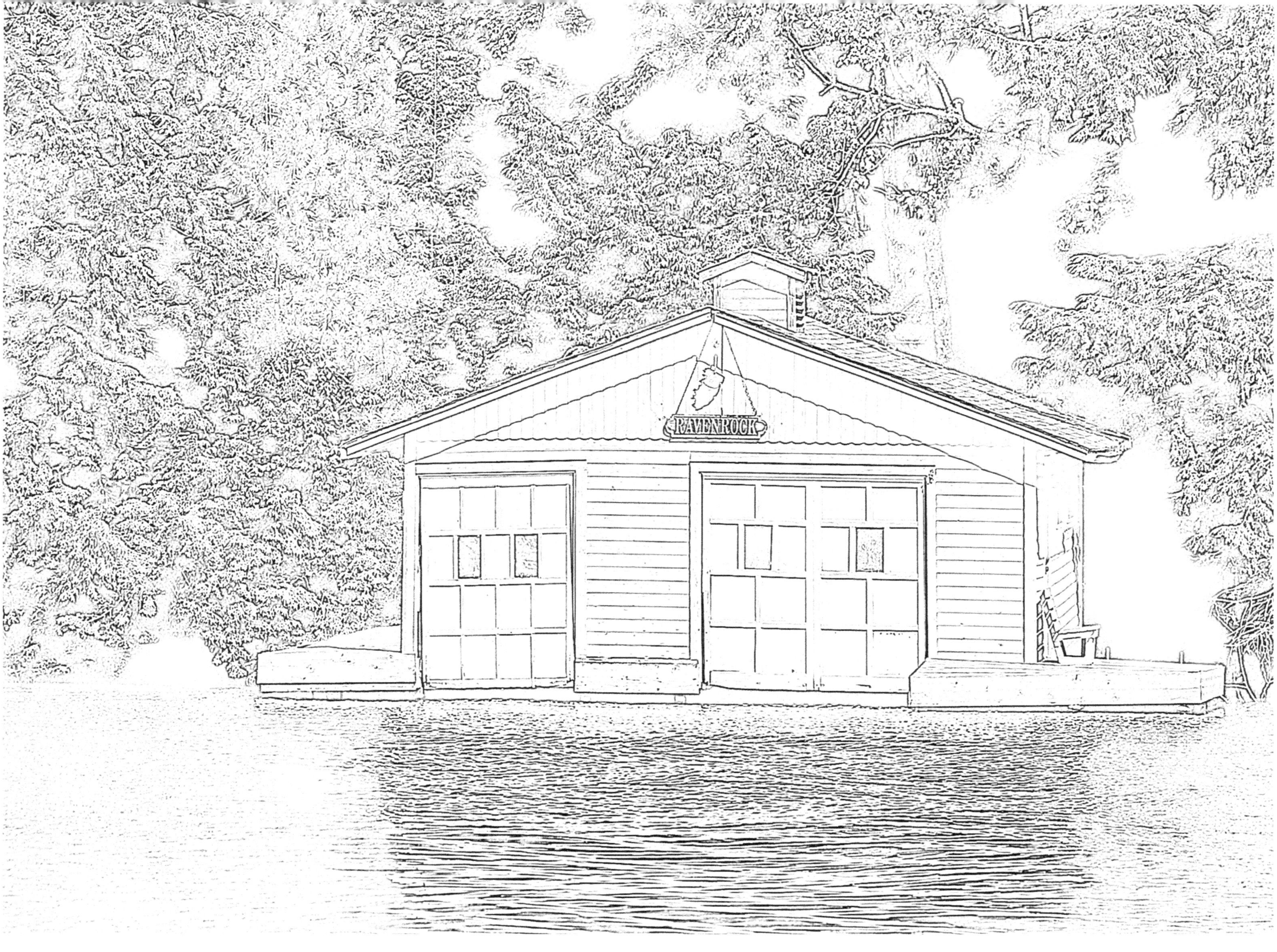
RAVENROCK

www.ingramcontent.com/pod-product-compliance
Lightning Source LLC
Chambersburg PA
CBHW060006230526
45472CB00008B/1975
9781720309321